Illustrated

Around The World In Eighty Days

Jules Verne

Retold by Alexander Swaby
Illustrated by Barry Davies

Contents

In 1872 Phileas Fogg discusses with some friends how the new railways across the world have transformed the speed of travel. They do not believe it to be possible but he wagers his entire fortune that he can travel right round the world in eighty days. His newly-appointed valet, Passepartout, who was hoping for a peaceful time in his new job, goes with him. They cross oceans, are chased by the police, ride an elephant, rescue a beautiful Indian girl from death and have many more fascinating adventures.

© Peter Haddock Limited
Bridlington, England

Chapter 1
Phileas and Passepartout Meet

Phileas Fogg lived in London on Savile Row in 1872. Although he was a regular member of the Reform Club, Phileas never seemed to attract attention and very little was known of him. He was never seen doing any work. He was not a lawyer, an artist or a scientist and, while he was certainly rich, he was not extravagant or greedy. He willingly gave money to worthy causes but always did it quietly.

In fact Phileas never spoke about himself although he could talk about any subject or place that came up, so he must have travelled widely. Did he have a wife or family? No one knew and that made people curious.

Phileas lived alone and never had visitors. He would walk briskly to the club each morning for breakfast and spend the rest of the day there, reading the newspaper and playing cards. He dined on the best food and wine and was served by the most attentive waiters. At the stroke of midnight Phileas left for his comfortable home.

On this particular morning, Phileas was waiting to interview a new valet. Being very particular, he had sacked his old valet for bringing shaving water at eighty-four degrees instead of eighty-six. At twenty past eleven a young man was shown in.

"You are French I believe," said Phileas, "and your name is John."

"If you like," said the newcomer, "but it's really Jean Passepartout, a very appropriate name considering the many jobs I've had — a travelling singer, a circus acrobat, a fireman in Paris and finally a valet here in London. Now I'm hoping for a quiet life so I can forget the name Passepartout."

"Passepartout suits me," replied Phileas. "You know my conditions. What time do you make it?"

"Twenty-two minutes past eleven," said Passepartout.

"You are slow."

"Pardon, monsieur, it is impossible," Passepartout protested.

"Four minutes slow," insisted Phileas. "It's not important, though now you know. From this moment you work for me."

Chapter 2
Passepartout is Convinced Phileas is Ideal

When he was younger, Passepartout had lived dangerously but all he wanted now was a quiet life. Since leaving Paris he had worked for ten gentlemen but all of them were too wild for his liking. Phileas, though, who never travelled or stayed out late, seemed the perfect employer.

"I've met wax dolls at Madame Tussauds livelier than Mr Fogg," thought Passepartout as he inspected the house. It was warm, light and clean. Everything was in its place, from the cellar to the attic. All round the house were electric bells and speaking tubes. He approved of his room on the second floor and noticed an electric clock, over the fireplace, identical to the one in Phileas's room and showing exactly the same time.

He found a card on the wall detailing precisely the day's schedule. Every task expected of him, from eight in the morning, was there. Tea and toast at eight twenty-three, shaving water at nine thirty-seven and so on until midnight. Even Phileas's suits and shoes were numbered with instructions to lay them out in turn through the year.

He rubbed his hands happily and a broad smile lit up his face.

"This is just what I've been looking for. We'll get on well together, Mr Fogg and me."

Chapter 3
An Expensive Conversation

Phileas left at precisely eleven thirty, leaving Passepartout to explore his new home, and walked to the Reform Club on Pall Mall. First he lunched on broiled fish, roast beef with mushrooms, a rhubarb and gooseberry tart and just a tiny piece of Cheshire cheese. Until dinner he read the newspapers from cover to cover while afterwards he settled down by the fire, with a few friends, for a game or two of cards. While playing, they discussed a daring robbery that was the talk of the town.

"It'll cost the bank thousands," said Stuart.

"Don't worry," said Ralph, a director of the bank, "we have detectives looking for him all across Europe and America." The robbery had happened while a teller had been distracted for a moment. Without protection from bars or guards, it had been easy for someone to walk off with fifty-five thousand pounds. The police discounted a professional band. A well-dressed gentleman had been seen in the bank where the crime occurred and his description had been circulated. "A two-thousand-pound reward ought to do the trick," said Ralph.

"But the world is so big, he could hide anywhere," said Stuart.

"It was once," Phileas said quietly.

"I agree with Mr Fogg," said Ralph. "Why, you can go round the world ten times quicker than a hundred years ago."

"So you think you could do it in three months?" asked Stuart.

"In eighty days," interrupted Phileas.

"That's true," John agreed. "With the new railway in India, the *Telegraph* estimates eighty days is possible."

"That's all very well, but what about bad weather and shipwrecks or rail accidents?"

"All included," said Phileas.

"Supposing there's a riot or a war. Supposing the tracks get pulled up or the train driver gets scalped. It's possible but not practical."

"All included," was Phileas's calm reply.

"I'd bet four thousand pounds you couldn't do it," challenged Stuart.

"I'd like nothing better but I warn you, it will be at your expense."

"Oh, this is nonsense," cried Ralph, "let's get on with the game."

Stuart started to deal then put down the pack.

"Right, Mr Fogg, I will bet you four thousand pounds."

"Calm down," said John, "it's only a joke."

"I mean it," insisted Stuart.

"Then let's make it twenty thousand," said Phileas.

"Twenty thousand!" cried Sullivan. "But you could lose by a day."

"The unforeseen does not exist," Phileas replied calmly. "I'll bet twenty thousand pounds against anyone that I can tour the world in eighty days or less. Do you accept?"

"We accept."

"Good," said Phileas. "The train leaves for Dover at a quarter to nine, this very evening. I'll take it."

He took out his diary.

"Today is October 2nd. I'll be back in this room on Saturday 21st December at a quarter to nine."

The clock struck seven but instead of rushing off to prepare, Phileas Fogg finished his game of whist.

Chapter 4
Passepartout is Astounded

Passepartout was surprised when his master returned home early.

"Pack a bag, Passepartout. We start for Dover and Calais in ten minutes."

A puzzled grin crossed Passepartout's face. "You are leaving home?"

"We're going round the world," replied Phileas.

Passepartout's eyebrows shot up. He seemed ready to collapse.

"Around the world!" he gasped.

"In eighty days, so we don't have a moment to lose. Pack a carpet-bag with two shirts and three pairs of socks each."

Passepartout was speechless. He went to his room and sank into a chair.

"So much for my quiet life."

Downstairs Phileas was waiting with a bound copy of Bradshaw's Continental Railway Timetable. When Passepartout came down Phileas handed him a second bag.

"Take good care of this, there are twenty thousand pounds in here."

They took a cab to Charing Cross and headed for the Dover train.

His friends from the Reform Club were waiting.

"You can check my passport to see that we have really made the journey," he told them.

"That won't be necessary," Ralph said. "We trust you."

As the train left the station Passepartout looked up in alarm.

"I've left the gas burning in my room."

"Young man," Phileas said coolly, "it will burn at your expense."

Chapter 5
Phileas's Reasons are Suspected

News of the wager spread quickly and before long everyone was arguing fiercely whether or not Phileas would succeed. The newspapers wrote page after page proving it could not be done. Only the *Telegraph* supported Phileas.

Most people thought it was madness. Fewer and fewer believed it was possible to cross India in three days and America in seven. Heavy bets were laid as though Phileas were in a horse race. At odds of two hundred and fifty to one only Lord Albemarle bet on Phileas, gambling five thousand pounds.

"If the thing is possible," he announced, "it ought to be an Englishman who does it first."

Across the city, at Scotland Yard, the Commissioner of Police received a telegram giving news of Phileas.

Suez to London
ROWAN, COMMISSIONER OF POLICE, SCOTLAND YARD

I've found the bank robber, Phileas Fogg. Send arrest warrant without delay to Bombay.

FIX, Detective.

Phileas's photograph from the Reform Club was carefully examined and compared with the robber's description. Of course. The wager was a ruse. Phileas had robbed the Bank of England and was using the trip as a way of escaping capture.

Chapter 6
Detective Fix Begins to Suspect Phileas

As soon as the robbery occurred, detectives were sent to cover the most likely get-away routes. Detective Fix had been ordered to Suez in Egypt, an important place thanks to the new canal that made it possible to reach the Indian Ocean in half the time it took to sail around the Cape.

Fix was a small, nervous man with bright eyes peering out from under constantly twitching eyebrows. He was pacing the quay anxiously, looking out for the steamer, *Magnolia*. With him was the British Consul.

"You say it's never late?" he asked for the twentieth time.

"No, Mr Fix," the consul replied patiently. "She reached Port Said yesterday from Italy and will be here on time. What I don't see, though, is how you hope to spot your man from the description you have. It could be almost any gentleman."

"You need a sixth sense to sniff out villains," said Fix. "If he's on board he won't slip through my fingers."

"I hope not," said the consul, as a series of sharp whistles announced the arrival of the steamer. "It was a terrible robbery."

Sailors, merchants and porters of all nationalities sprang into action. A dozen boats pushed off to meet her. In the pale sunlight the *Magnolia* dropped anchor and Fix took up position to watch the passengers disembark.

"How long will she stop in Suez?" he asked the consul.

"Four hours, just long enough to take on coal for the next leg to Bombay."

As Fix scrutinised each passenger leaving the ship one of them pushed his way through the crowd and politely asked if he could point out the way to the consulate. Instinctively, Fix took the passport and read the description.

"Is this yours?" he asked.

"No," replied Passepartout, "it's my master's. He's still on board and doesn't want to be disturbed."

"There's the consulate, on the corner," Fix told him, "but I'm afraid he'll have to go in person."

Bowing gratefully, Passepartout went to break the bad news to Phileas.

Chapter 7
Phileas's Passport is No Help to Fix

Fix and the consul were waiting for Phileas to appear to have his passport stamped.

"I won't be sorry to see the rascal arrested," said the consul, "but surely robbers don't like to leave trails and he's not forced to have his passport countersigned."

"If he's as clever as I think," Fix told the consul, "he'll come. I'd like you, though, not to stamp his passport and to keep him here until I can get a warrant for his arrest."

"I'm sorry," said the consul, "but that's not . . ."

He was interrupted by a knock as Phileas and Passepartout entered. The consul examined the passport Phileas gave him.

"You know you don't need a visa for Bombay, Mr Fogg."

"I know that but I wish to prove I came via Suez," said Phileas as he left.

"Well," asked Fix, "don't you agree he fits the description?"

"He could do," the consul conceded reluctantly, "but . . ."

"I'll make certain," said Fix, running after Passepartout. "The manservant is French and you know they love talking."

Meanwhile, back on the steamer, Phileas looked at a table he had drawn in his diary where he logged his daily progress, recording losses or gains. Here in Suez, after six and a half days, he had neither lost nor gained.

Chapter 8
Passepartout Gives Fix Encouragement

"Well, my friend," said Fix, when he found Passepartout on the quayside, "you like the view?"

"Our journey is so fast, monsieur, that it all seems like a dream," Passepartout replied. "Just think, here we are in Suez, in Egypt, in Africa."

"You're in a hurry then?"

"I'm not," Passepartout told Fix, "but my master is. Could you show me where I can buy some shirts? We left so quickly we came without them. But please, not too far away. I mustn't miss the steamer."

"Don't worry," Fix told him. "It's only twelve o'clock."

Passepartout pulled out his big watch. "Twelve!" he exclaimed. "It's only ten o'clock."

"You're still on London time. Remember that as you move east, you have to adjust your watch each day."

"Never," insisted Passepartout, failing to understand Fix's explanation.

As Fix showed Passepartout the shop, he questioned him about Phileas.

"Where is your master heading?"

"Always straight ahead," said Passepartout. "He's going round the world — in eighty days. He says it's a wager but I think there's something else."

"Mr Fogg is certainly a character. Is he rich?"

22

"I'll say," Passepartout told him eagerly. "In his bag he has twenty thousand pounds in brand-new notes and he's offered the captain a reward if he gets to Bombay ahead of schedule."

"Have you known Mr Fogg long?" Fix asked.

"Why no. I joined him the very day we left London."

You can imagine the effect these replies had on the already-suspicious Detective Fix.

"There's one thing that worries me though," Passepartout moaned. "My gas burner. Burning day and night, I've calculated that it's costing me two shillings every twenty-four hours, sixpence more than I get paid!"

Fix wasn't listening to Passepartout's troubles. He was now convinced he had his man. Hurrying back to the consulate he passed on what he'd learnt.

"Send a telegram quickly to Scotland Yard. I'm taking the steamer to Bombay where I intend arresting Mr Phileas Fogg."

Chapter 9
The Journey to Bombay

On board the *Magnolia* was a lively bunch of travellers — soldiers, government officials and their wives — making the ship ring with music and dancing. But regardless of what party was being organised, or what majestic sight there was to see, Phileas remained unmoved, seldom even bothering to go on deck. Just as he did at the Reform Club, Phileas spent his time eating heartily and playing the occasional hand of whist.

Despite his earlier worries, Passepartout was rather enjoying himself. He ate well, avoided seasickness and took an interest in everything he saw. He was also pleased to meet Fix on deck, especially when Fix bought him a drink or two. At every opportunity the detective worked questions about Phileas into their conversation but learnt no more than he already knew.

Day and night, fair or foul, the *Magnolia* ploughed on under the encouragement of the reward Phileas had promised. By the time they reached Aden they were fifteen hours ahead of schedule. By the first sighting of India's mysterious coastline, Phileas recorded in his diary that they had made up two full days since leaving London.

Chapter 10
Passepartout Loses His Shoes

The plan, on reaching Bombay, was to take the eight o'clock train to Calcutta across the other side of the continent. Phileas went straight to the station ignoring, as usual, the wonderful sights and sounds. At the inn he declined what the landlord described as rabbit but which Phileas suspected was more likely to be cat.

Fix was also busy. At the police station he asked if the warrant had arrived, only to be disappointed. He failed to persuade the local police to issue a warrant but felt sure Phileas would stay long enough for his to arrive.

Passepartout went to buy fresh shirts and shoes. He stopped to watch a colourful Parsee festival wind its way through the streets. As the procession disappeared, Passepartout saw a splendid temple. Not having learnt the local rules, he did not know that it was forbidden for Christians to enter, or even worse, to do so wearing shoes.

He went in and was soon lost in admiration. A moment later, Passepartout found himself thrown to the ground by three priests wrestling off his shoes. Swinging fists and feet, the agile Frenchman finally wriggled free and made it to the door. But when he reached the station he had lost his hat, coat and shoes as well as the parcel of fresh clothing. Phileas was not amused.

Fix, on the other hand, had a plan. An offence had been committed on Indian soil and he now had a reason for arresting his man.

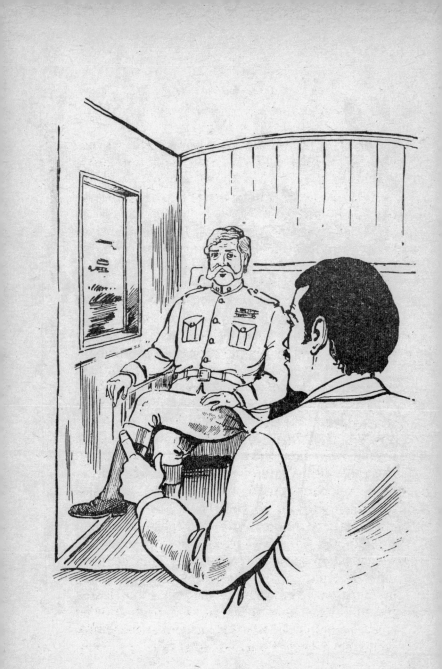

Chapter 11
Strange and Expensive Transport

The train pulled out exactly on time. Phileas was sharing a carriage with Sir Francis Cromarty, a general about to rejoin his troops.

An hour out of Bombay they reached a branch line going south.

"A few years ago, Mr Fogg," the general said, "you would have been delayed here; probably long enough to lose your bet."

"How's that?" asked Phileas.

"Because the track stopped at these mountains and passengers had to cross them by pony."

"That wouldn't have delayed me in the least," said Phileas. "I've planned for such problems."

"But Mr Fogg, look at your valet's trouble in the temple. He could have been arrested."

"If so he'd have been punished and sent back to England," replied Phileas. "But I don't see how that would have slowed down my progress."

Hour after hour the train sped on past villages, minarets, farms and rivers. They passed battlefields and the kingdoms of rajahs and saw elephants working in forests.

At the first opportunity Passepartout bought some Indian slippers to replace his lost shoes. He was now convinced they would keep on the move until they had circled the world and felt deeply involved with the wager, worrying about losing through delays and accidents. His flesh crawled when he thought of how his incident at the temple could have been Phileas's downfall.

"What time do you make it, Passepartout?" the general asked.

"Three in the morning, sir," came the obviously wrong reply. His watch was still stubbornly set for English time.

Unexpectedly, the train stopped.

"All passengers out, please."

Passepartout went to investigate and returned with the alarming news that there was no more railway. The track had not been finished. They complained loudly to the conductor but he simply told them that regular passengers knew they had to make their own way from there on. By the time they looked for transport, all the wagons, ponies and carriages had been snapped up.

"I shall walk," announced Phileas.

"I think I have a better plan," Passepartout told them, leading the way to an enclosure.

"An elephant!" exclaimed Phileas. "Just the ticket." But despite offering twenty pounds an hour to hire it, the owner flatly refused. Phileas then tried to buy it outright for one thousand pounds. The general begged Phileas to think what he was doing, offering such a fortune. But the success of his wager was at stake. Up and up went the price until at two thousand pounds, the Indian gave in.

"What a price," cried Passepartout, "for an elephant!"

Finding a guide and equipping the elephant took less time than it had to buy it and soon, with Phileas and the general in baskets on either side of the elephant, Passepartout perched high on its back and the driver on its neck, the most expensive part of the journey began.

Chapter 12
Journey Across India

None of them could have dreamt how uncomfortable the ride was to be. After two hours the travellers were delighted when the elephant stopped to rest.

The countryside was very difficult and the inhabitants unfriendly. Wherever he could, the guide avoided the locals. That night they camped in a deserted bungalow. They fell asleep so quickly that not even the chattering monkeys disturbed them.

By four the next day they were only a few miles away from the station when the elephant became restless. So far there had been no sign of trouble but now a confused murmuring came through the trees. The guide scouted ahead. A party of Brahmin was coming their way.

"They mustn't see us," he told them.

Hiding in a thicket, ready to flee if they were spotted, they watched the procession approach. The sound of the tambourines and cymbals filled the air. First came priests in tall head-dresses and lace robes. Then came the village folk, chanting monotonously and leading a large wagon, the huge wheels of which had spokes carved like snakes. On the cart stood a hideous statue with four arms, a dull-red body and wild hair. Its tongue stuck out and its lips were stained scarlet with berry juice. The statue was standing on the shape of a headless giant.

"That's Kali," whispered the general, "goddess of love and death."

Behind the wagon a young woman, so fair she could have been European, was led by some of the Brahmin. She was stumbling at every step, her neck and arms loaded in jewels and gold chains. Following the unhappy girl were powerful guards with murderous swords and long, fancy pistols in their belts. Some of them were carrying the body of an old man laid on palm branches. He wore the clothes of a rajah — the finest silk robes and a pearl-encrusted turban. At the rear of the procession were more musicians and fanatical fakirs.

"The girl is a human sacrifice," the general explained. "She is the wife of the dead prince and will be burned with him."

"Devils." Phileas was shocked beyond belief. "Why has this dreadful sort of thing not been stopped; the poor wretch, being burnt alive."

"If she weren't," explained the general, "her family would treat her badly. They'd shave her head, ignore her and feed her on scraps. Unless she becomes an outcast, she has no choice."

The guide spoke up.

"This is not a normal funeral. Her sacrifice is not voluntary. She is drugged with opium and going against her will." The guide told Aouda's story. Born into a wealthy Bombay family, she had been well educated but when orphaned had been forced to marry the ageing rajah against her will.

The procession moved on. Leading the elephant out of the thicket the guide urged them to leave quickly. Phileas didn't move.

"I have twelve hours to spare," he said, "so why don't we rescue her?"

Chapter 13
Fortune Favours the Brave

Although the project was obviously dangerous, Phileas had not hesitated for a second. Neither did Passepartout, who felt that Phileas might have a heart after all.

The group hid close to the temple where the dreadful sacrifice was to be held at dawn the next day. When night fell the guide led them silently towards the building. They passed a high stack of wood. On top lay the dead rajah. All around the temple the villagers lay in a drunken sleep. But at the temple soldiers guarded the door, swords shining in the torch-light. Unless they slept, it would be impossible to enter through the front. Yet, although they waited patiently till midnight, the soldiers showed no sign of relaxing. Another plan was necessary.

The temple was a simple construction of soft bricks and timber. Passepartout decided to try making a hole in the wall. With the guide he slipped around the side and began to loosen the mortar between the bricks. They soon had a hole started but before they could finish a loud cry came from inside followed by others outside. Had they been seen? Afraid of being caught, they melted into the forest. Guards appeared at the rear, sent by a commander who suspected attack from all sides. Their work had not been found but could not continue. Disappointed, Passepartout and the general felt they had no

choice but to leave. Phileas calmly reminded them
that they still had twelve hours before their train
left for Allahabad.

Settling down once more to wait patiently for something to happen, Passepartout climbed a tree. From his position, high on a branch, a plan flashed into his head.

Minute by minute, the night lost its blackness. The songs and tambourines began again. The crowd grew excited as the temple doors were thrown open. The procession made its way to the funeral pyre. Now totally unconscious, the poor girl was laid by her dead husband and burning torches were tossed on to the oil-soaked wood. Suddenly the whole scene changed. A terrified cry went up. The Indians threw themselves flat to the ground. The old rajah was not dead. Like a ghost, he rose with his wife, Aouda, in his arms. Surrounded by clouds of smoke, he climbed from the pyre and walked through the horrified crowd. In good, English fashion, Phileas and the general stood respectfully to attention and bowed their heads. The corpse drew near and whispered,

"Come on, let's get out of here!"

They were amazed to see Passepartout under the turban. His bravery had saved the young girl from death. A moment later, now with five passengers on board, the elephant was once again on its way, running as fast as the guide could encourage it.

Chapter 14
The Valley of the Ganges

For an hour, as the elephant crashed on through the jungle, Passepartout could not stop laughing at what he had done. The general had shaken his hand vigorously and even Phileas had managed a brisk, "Well done!"

Aouda, still drugged, was wrapped in a travelling blanket. Not even the bumping could wake her as she slept in one of the baskets. What was to happen to her? She was hardly safe anywhere. If ever Aouda was caught, she would be sure to die.

They reached Allahabad with two hours to spare. At the station it only remained to say goodbye to the guide.

"Parsee," said Phileas, "you've been paid for your work but not your loyalty. The elephant is yours."

"But he's worth a fortune, your honour."

"Take him," insisted Phileas, "and I'll still be in your debt."

Passepartout gave the elephant a leaving present of sugar lumps and the next minute found himself high in the air lifted by the elephant's massive trunk.

The train was well on its way to Calcutta by the time Aouda fully regained her senses. Surrounded by strangers Aouda could hardly believe her ears as the general told her what had happened in the past twenty-four hours.

With tears in her eyes she thanked them as well as she could. Not knowing what to do with herself, when she heard where Phileas was heading, she accepted his offer to go with them hoping to find a distant relative in Hong Kong.

At the desolate town of Benares the general left to meet his troops. If he expected a warm goodbye from Phileas he was unlucky. A quick handshake was all he got, although Passepartout and Aouda seemed sadder to see him go.

Through the valley of the Ganges River the train passed fields of wheat and barley, crossed jungles thick with vines and straddled swamps teaming with green alligators and turtles.

On and on the train sped, until at seven the next day, having crossed the whole of India, it finally reached Calcutta. Phileas's diary entry for October 25th simply recorded that he had reached Calcutta on schedule — neither ahead nor behind. The two days he had gained travelling to Bombay had been lost but it is unlikely that Phileas regretted that in any way.

Chapter 15
More Money is Spent

Phileas and Passepartout helped Aouda from the carriage. The plan was to go straight to the ship and get settled immediately but, just as they were leaving the station, a burly policeman stopped them.

"Are you Mr Phileas Fogg and is this your manservant?" he asked.

"That's so," replied Phileas.

"Then I must ask you to follow me."

For twenty minutes they drove through slums and past palaces until finally, reaching a more modest house, they were led inside and put into a barred room.

"You'll see the judge at eight thirty," the policeman told them as he left.

At half past eight they were taken to a larger room where Judge Obadiah was to try their case. A door at the rear of the room opened and in walked three Indian priests. In a loud voice the clerk read out the charge of violating a sacred place.

"How do you plead?" asked the judge.

"We are guilty, sir."

"You admit it?" the judge said, in surprise.

"I do, sir, but I want to ask what they intended to do to this poor girl at the temple?"

The priests looked at each other in confusion.

"That's right," shouted Passepartout. "We stopped them from burning an innocent widow."

"What widow?" Judge Obadiah spluttered. "Burn? In Bombay? We're talking of violating a temple and here are the shoes to prove it."

"My shoes," cried Passepartout. Suddenly all became clear. They were talking about Passepartout's adventure in Bombay. Fix had seen his chance and persuaded the priests to lodge a complaint. They had followed Passepartout to Calcutta, in search of compensation.

"You admit it then," said the judge. "In that case I sentence you to fifteen days in jail and a fine of three hundred pounds! And, Mr Fogg, I sentence you to one week in jail and a one-hundred-and-fifty-pound fine as you are responsible for the actions of your employees."

Fix rubbed his hands in glee. Now he had plenty of time to get Phileas's arrest warrant.

"Can I offer bail?" Phileas asked the judge.

"Yes, you can," he was told. "The amount will be one thousand pounds each, which will be returned to you when you leave prison."

Out of the bag came another bundle of notes from a store getting dangerously low.

"Come on," said Phileas to Passepartout, grabbing his precious shoes. Fix followed, not thinking for a second that Phileas would leave behind two thousand pounds. But at eleven o'clock he could not believe his eyes when he saw them board the *Rangoon,* bound for Hong Kong. Fix swore.

"He can't go on for ever," he thought. "The money must run out soon."

He was correct. What with buying tickets and

an elephant as well as paying assorted bribes, bails and fines, Phileas had already spent over five thousand pounds.

Chapter 16
Fix Does Not Understand What is Being Said

The *Rangoon* was as fast as the *Magnolia* but not as comfortable but with a journey of only ten to twelve days they would manage well enough.

Aouda got to know Phileas better. Each day he would see her two or three times, asking if she had everything she needed.

Fix, in the meantime, had managed to get a berth on the *Rangoon* and spent all his time in his cabin, plotting how he could arrest Phileas. He had slipped up twice already and if it happened again in Hong Kong that would be the end of his reputation. Whatever it took or cost, he was determined to stop Phileas. If it came to the worst, he decided, he would confide in Passepartout. He was sure the valet was not part of the robbery and would be shocked to find his master was a thief. He even wondered if he could use Aouda in some way. Where had she come from? Were they married? Was there a scandal somewhere? Before he could plan further he had to question Passepartout.

The next day, before the ship was due to stop at Singapore, he went on deck and pretended to see Passepartout for the first time. Poor Fix was so disappointed when he learnt of the rescue and the very honourable way Phileas and Aouda had met.

Chapter 17
Singapore to Hong Kong

The reappearance of Fix began to puzzle Passepartout. Was it coincidence or was Fix following them? He racked his brains and eventually hit on an explanation that fitted the facts. If Fix was following them, he must be a spy hired by the Reform Club to check on Phileas.

He decided not to tell Phileas in case it hurt his feelings. But he would make it difficult for Fix and let him know his game was rumbled.

"You're in a big hurry?" Fix asked Passepartout one day as the Frenchman gazed out to sea. "I suppose Mr Fogg wants to catch the steamer to Yokohama?"

"Certainly."

"So you believe in his round-the-world story then?" Fix asked.

"You're a sly dog," said Passepartout with a wink.

This unexpected comment from Passepartout puzzled the detective. What could Passepartout mean? Had he been found out?

Next day Passepartout went further.

"Shall we lose you when we reach Hong Kong? Or will you be going on to America? And of course, from there it's only a short step back to Europe."

Fix looked for clues in Passepartout's face.

"It's always possible," was his cautious reply.

Was the game up? Had Passepartout found him out and told Phileas? He decided that if he could not arrest Phileas in Hong Kong he would have no choice but to tell Passepartout exactly what he was doing. If Passepartout knew of the robbery, he would warn Phileas and Fix would fail. But if Passepartout was innocent then it would be in his interests to help Fix.

Chapter 18
Everyone is Busy

On the last few days of their voyage, luck went against them. A huge storm blew up, forcing the captain to take in all the sails. Phileas took the news they would be delayed by twenty hours as calmly as always, even though it meant they would miss their Yokohama connection.

Fix was delighted. The storm had at last given him the chance to arrest this man. Although the foul weather made him seasick, Fix prayed for it to continue.

Eventually, as always happens, the weather changed again and was once more fine. But even at full speed, with all sails set, the *Rangoon* would still be twenty-four hours behind schedule. Perhaps, though, Phileas did have an angel looking after him. As they reached the China coastline, a pilot came on board to guide them through the tricky waters and into harbour. As calmly as you like, Phileas asked him if he knew when the next boat to Yokohama would sail.

"The *Carnatic* sails at high tide tomorrow," the pilot replied.

"Shouldn't she have left today?"

"Yes sir," said the pilot, "but they had to do some repairs on the boiler, so she was delayed for a while."

Once more Phileas was back on schedule. The ship across the Pacific Ocean, from Yokohama to San Francisco, could not leave until the

Carnatic arrived, so even if he was a few hours late he would still catch his connection.

In Hong Kong Phileas had sixteen hours to find Aouda's relative. Phileas set out for the Stock Exchange where rich men meet. Yes, they had heard of him, but not for two years. Having made a fortune, he had decided to retire. No-one knew for sure but they thought he was now in Holland! When she heard the news, poor Aouda was heartbroken.

"What can I do, Mr Fogg?" she asked.

"It's simple," said Phileas, "you have to come with us to Europe. Passepartout, go and book *three* cabins on the *Carnatic!*"

Chapter 19
Passepartout is Too Interested in Phileas

Hong Kong is a tiny island off the coast of China that Britain turned into a very busy trading centre in and out of China.

Reaching the docks, Passepartout saw his old friend, Fix, not looking at all happy.

Fix was actually annoyed because the arrest warrant still had not caught up with him.

"Why, Mr Fix," said Passepartout, pretending surprise at finding the detective there. "Don't tell me we have your company to America?"

They booked their cabins and learnt that the ship was to leave that night after all. In desperation, Fix decided he had no alternative but to confide in Passepartout. He led the Frenchman to an inn where men not only drank but smoked opium, a terrible drug that made life miserable for millions of Chinese.

"I need to have a serious talk with you," he hissed. "What I have to say concerns your master. You've guessed who I am so I'll tell you everything."

"Let me tell you," said Passepartout loyally, "that those fellows have wasted their money unnecessarily."

"Unless you know how much is involved."

"Of course I do," said Passepartout. "Twenty thousand pounds."

"Fifty-five, more like," Fix told him.

"Mr Fogg has risked fifty-five thousand! All

the more reason for not losing then.''

Fix pushed Passepartout back in his chair.

"If I succeed, I get two thousand. And if you help me to make Mr Fogg miss the ship, you can have half.''

"But that's terrible," cried Passepartout. "Not only do those men not trust my master, they now want to put obstacles in his way."

"What men?" asked Fix, confused.

"The Reform Club members, of course. And you are their spy."

It suddenly dawned on Fix that Passepartout knew nothing at all.

"Listen to me," he said to Passepartout and told him the whole story of the robbery and his assignment to find the thief.

Of course, Passepartout protested that Mr Fogg was a gentleman and totally honest.

"Do you want to be arrested as an accomplice?" Fix threatened. "You must help me keep Mr Fogg here and I'll share my reward."

"Never," said Passepartout bravely. "Even if what you say is true, Mr Fogg is my employer and has treated me very well. I can't betray him like that. I refuse!"

Fix tried to calm things down.

"Just consider things," he said, "and let's have a drink."

Well into their second bottle of port, Passepartout again calmed down. On the table lay several opium pipes, waiting for customers. Under the influence of the drink, Fix was able to slip one between Passepartout's lips and light it. Only a few puffs were needed to make Passepartout's eyes feel heavy and, in a second, his head fell on the table.

Chapter 20
Phileas and Fix Come Face to Face

In the hotel the next morning, when Passepartout failed to answer his call, Phileas packed his bag, called Aouda and ordered a rickshaw to take them to the docks only to find that the *Carnatic* had already left.

Detective Fix had been waiting for Phileas. Walking up to him he asked politely,

"Pardon me, I was hoping to see your manservant."

"Do you know where he is?" Aouda asked. "We think he may have sailed on the *Carnatic*."

"You too are going to Yokohama?" said Fix. "I hear the repairs were finished early and the ship left last night. We're stuck for some time."

"In a harbour this size," said Phileas, "there must be another vessel we can find."

"Pardon me, your honour," said a sailor, "I've got a boat to hire. A pilot boat — the best there is. She'll do eight or nine knots."

But when he heard Phileas's destination the sailor spluttered in disbelief.

"I'm sorry," said the sailor, "but that's impossible."

"I'll offer you two hundred pounds a day and two hundred pounds if I reach Yokohama by the fourteenth at the latest."

The pilot walked away a little and gazed out to sea. He was tempted but knew the dangers.

"Tell you what," he said, after a while, "you'd

never make Yokohama; it's too far but there is another way." The sailor explained that the ship they wanted started its journey from Shanghai. By going there, they would avoid the most dangerous seas and still catch the ship.

"Here's two hundred pounds in advance," said Phileas. "Be ready in an hour." Turning to Fix he asked,

"Would you like to join us? In the meantime I have to find Passepartout."

That was easier said than done. Despite visiting the police and the French consulate Phileas found no clues to his disappearance.

At three o'clock the skipper, John Bunsby, and the crew of the pilot boat *Tankadere* were ready. All of them were deeply sunburnt from years of sailing on the treacherous China Sea.

After the *Magnolia* and *Rangoon* this little boat seemed too tiny to cross the seas. She was only a twenty-tonner but her timbers were varnished and her brass gleamed. Instead of one cabin each, there was just a single cabin below decks with simple bunks around the wall and the whole area was lit by one swinging, oil lamp. Here, Phileas and his party, as well as the crew, would all have to sleep.

Taking a last look towards land, in the hope of spotting Passepartout, Phileas and Aouda sat on deck as the *Tankadere* put to sea.

Bothered by a bad conscience at taking a ride from the man he was trying to capture, Fix kept to himself as much as was possible on such a tiny boat.

Chapter 21
Danger on the High Seas

For a boat of only twenty tons, the eight hundred miles to Shanghai were dangerous at the best of times. But in November, the winter storms were beginning to blow.

Phileas watched the crew at work. The wind grew stronger and it would have been better to take in some of the sails but they stayed up and the boat fairly flew along.

The boat kept close to the coast, where the currents were more favourable. After two days the log showed two hundred and twenty miles but then they entered rougher waters and the wind strengthened. At dawn next day it was really blowing. Captain Bunsby spoke quietly to his crew. They all agreed. There was a typhoon coming up.

"From the north or the south?" asked Phileas. Finding that it was south, he simply said it would take them all the quicker.

A single, small sail, made from heavy canvas, was the only one left up. All they could do now was wait. Bunsby suggested the passengers go below but no one went. With the boat bouncing around, it was more comfortable on deck. The worst weather hit them by eight o'clock. The boat was lifted like a feather by waves so large they would have crushed a weaker boat.

So far the captain had been able to hold the correct course for Shanghai but now, instead of

going with the waves, the boat had to sail across them and began rolling wildly. Wave after wave crashed into them without relief. Finally, Bunsby could take no more.

"I think we should head for port," he shouted above the wind and rain.

"I think so too," Phileas agreed. "Let's head for Shanghai." Phileas had no intention of turning around and was insisting they go on.

"So be it, your honour," said the captain.

By noon, the tempest lost its power. The sun peeped through the clouds and the seas calmed.

Every sail was once again set but with a hundred miles to go in only one day, the captain began to fear he would lose his bonus.

Time slipped by and so did the miles. By noon the next day the little boat was within forty-five miles of its target. The crew tried every trick to catch the least breath of wind. By six o'clock they were just ten miles from Shanghai River. At that moment, the lookout spotted smoke. Soon, a tall, black funnel announced the American steamer was leaving for Yokohama dead on time.

"Signal her," said Phileas calmly. A small brass cannon was loaded. "Hoist your flag too," Phileas told him.

"Fire!" ordered Phileas. The boom of the little cannon filled the air.

Chapter 22
Passepartout Finds it Helps to Have Money

When the *Carnatic* left Hong Kong, two of the three cabins ordered by Phileas were empty. The next morning, a bleary-eyed Passepartout staggered out of the third. Shortly after Fix had left the opium den, two waiters carried Passepartout over to the beds reserved for smokers. With dreams of ships chasing through his head, he woke up briefly and made it to the door. No more than a few metres away, he was able to stumble on to the steamer before collapsing into sleep once more.

As he recovered he worried what Phileas and Aouda would think of the way he had let them down. Then he remembered what Fix had told him and realised it was not his fault.

As well as he could, Passepartout staggered around the rolling steamer looking for Phileas. He was nowhere to be found. When he asked an officer and discovered that neither was on board Passepartout was thunderstruck. It all came back. Phileas did not know the departure time had changed. He was stranded in Hong Kong — his fortune lost.

After his first panic, Passepartout calmed down and began to think. His passage was paid to Japan, which was just as well, as he had not even a penny in his pocket. There was nothing left to do but make the best of it.

The steamer arrived in Japan on schedule. Passepartout left the ship and ventured into the streets, crowded with Dutch, Americans, Chinese and English, feeling as much at home as a Hottentot would. The Japanese district he came to next looked much different — fir and cedar groves, bamboo and reeds, bridges hidden by mist and strange temples where priests played dreary-sounding drums while soldiers strutted in fancy uniforms. Passepartout saw working-men with shaved heads and straw sandals, ladies in tight dresses took tiny steps on tiny, wooden shoes, their teeth blackened fashionably. Away from the houses Passepartout passed strangely-grinning scarecrows and weeping willows in which herons stood on one leg.

Although he had had a good breakfast Passepartout was getting hungry. He saw some violets and remembered how he used to eat them. But these flowers had no smell or taste and he moved on. At night-fall Passepartout returned to the native quarter. The streets were lit by colourful, paper lanterns. Girls danced while astronomers showed towns-people the moon through telescopes. Back near the harbour Passepartout gladly fell asleep, watching fishermen work by lantern light.

Chapter 23
Passepartout's Long Nose

The next morning, still famished, Passepartout decided he would try busking to earn money. Dressed in fancy, European clothes, though, he wondered if he did not look too wealthy to be a street singer. If he could sell his clothes he could buy more suitable peasant clothing and still have money for breakfast.

Wearing an old Japanese coat and a faded turban he settled down to enjoy half a bird and a little rice. Feeling much better, although once again out of cash, he thought of another plan. Perhaps he could work his passage across the Pacific as a ship's cook or a servant. But who would hire him? What references could he give? Just then he saw a clown carrying an enormous placard, announcing that a Japanese Acrobatic Troupe, known as the Long Noses, was about to perform for the last time before travelling to America. If he could join the troupe he could get to America at their expense.

Passepartout followed the clown and soon found himself outside a large cabin, the property of the Hon. William Batulcar — manager of the Long Noses. Finding Mr Batulcar, Passepartout asked him if he needed a manservant. "I already have two," he was told, "but if you can pull a funny face you could be a clown." Mr Batulcar thought further, "You look strong. Can you sing as well? And stand on your head with a ball

spinning on your left foot and a sword balanced on the right?''

"I expect so," said Passepartout.

"Then you can become a Long Nose!"

Having no time to practise anything, Passepartout's job was to be in the bottom row of the massive, human pyramid that would end the show.

It must be admitted that the Japanese are master acrobats. The performance was a real eye-opener to Passepartout. One man juggled lighted candles, another wrote words in blue smoke while others imitated butterflies. Someone did a trick with spinning tops, managing to get them to balance on the edges of sword blades, wires and even human hair, stretched across the stage.

So many wonderful acts followed each other until it was time for the amazing finale performed by the peculiar Long Noses. They had earned the name from their unusual habit of wearing false noses, made from bamboo, anything up to two or three metres long. Some were curved, some straight and others ribbed. A few even had warts. Somehow they were fastened to the acrobats' real noses tightly enough for them to perform tricks while balancing on them.

After a routine of jumps and somersaults, the pyramid was to be formed. Not on each others' shoulders, in the normal way, but on their noses. Because of his inexperience and strength, poor Passepartout was on the very bottom, taking the weight of all those on top. Inside his costume, with multi-coloured wings and ridiculous nose, he felt he had made a terrible mistake. On stage

71

he took his place with the others and in a moment the pyramid was one, two, three and then four layers high, to the very roof of the building. The orchestra was playing a crescendo when the pyramid began to topple. One of the lower Noses was moving and the pyramid was badly unbalanced.

"Master, my master," cried Passepartout, spotting Phileas and Aouda in the audience.

"You're here then," replied Phileas calmly. "Come on, young man. To the ship with you." They left Mr Batulcar grasping a handful of pound notes given to him by Phileas in compensation for the trouble they had caused.

Chapter 24
Across the Pacific Ocean

Phileas's plan with the flag had worked. The Yokohama steamer came to investigate, giving Phileas the chance to get aboard.

Once in Japan he lost no time visiting the *Carnatic,* learning that Passepartout had indeed been on board. But with only a few hours before his ship sailed, where would he start to look? Was it a guardian angel that led him to Mr Batulcar's? He would never have recognised Passepartout but Passepartout saw him, crashing the pyramid but re-uniting the team.

Aouda quickly told Passepartout their story.

When he heard that Fix had actually travelled with them he went cold with anger. But instead of telling Phileas the truth he put his disappearance down to drunkenness.

The journey to San Francisco was expected to take twenty-one days. Add the time to cross America and the Atlantic Ocean and Phileas should be back home with a day to spare.

The day they were exactly halfway around the world Passepartout discovered that his watch was once again correct, giving the same time as the ship's clock. What Passepartout did not realise was that although both said nine o'clock, the ship's was nine in the morning while his watch thought it was nine in the evening. He still did not understand why time is different in other parts of the world even though Fix and the general had tried to explain.

Incidentally, where was Fix? It will not surprise you to hear that he was on board. Amazingly, Fix had recognised Passepartout, even under his

'Long-Nose' disguise, and was keeping well out of his way. However, it was not possible to stay in his cabin for three weeks so it was only a matter of time until Passepartout spotted him. When he did, Passepartout attacked Fix like a terrier, knocking him off his feet and giving him a good hiding.

"Have you finished?" Fix asked. "Then let me talk to you. It's in Mr Fogg's interest."

They sat by the rails away from other passengers.

"Up till now," Fix said, "I've been against Mr Fogg, but from now on, I'm for him."

"So you finally believe he's innocent?"

"Not a bit of it," Fix replied coldly. "I think he's a terrible villain and I want to see him back on English soil — where I can arrest him! So," asked Fix, "are we friends?"

"Not friends but allies perhaps," said Passepartout reluctantly.

Reaching San Francisco on December 3rd, Phileas recorded that he had neither gained nor lost a single day.

Chapter 25
A Slight Glimpse of San Francisco

It was seven in the morning when Phileas, Passepartout and Aouda set foot on the floating quays that were their first sight of America. All around were ships bringing goods from Peru and the Pacific Islands.

The travellers had a whole day to spare. Driving to the International Hotel, Passepartout marvelled at the magnificent city. Less than twenty-five years ago it had been a paradise for outlaws. In those days San Francisco was ruled with the gun. But now, instead of gun fights in the streets, there were shops as fine as any in London, Paris or New York.

After breakfast Phileas headed for the British consulate to have his passport stamped. Passepartout asked if it would not be wiser to stock up with rifles or Colt revolvers. He had been listening to terrifying stories of attacks by Sioux and Pawnee Red Indians. Phileas thought it unnecessary but told Passepartout to do as he thought best.

No sooner were they out on the bright, sunny street, than Phileas and Aouda, by the greatest of chances, bumped into Fix. He seemed astounded to hear they had crossed the Pacific on the very same steamer and were, incredibly, heading towards Europe too. Fix asked if he could travel with them and Phileas agreed.

After a while they found themselves

surrounded by a crowd, growing larger by the second. Men carrying banners or hanging streamers from windows seemed to be supporting one of two people.

"It's a political meeting," said Fix. "There could be trouble."

They moved to the top of some steps. The crowd was so large that they must be electing someone very important — a senator perhaps. A show of hands went up and the crowd began to move. Before they knew it, Phileas and his companions were once again swallowed up. Fists flew and banners became weapons. The centre of the riot moved up the steps towards them.

"I really think we should leave," a worried Fix repeated. But before they could move, they found themselves between two rival gangs attacking each other with rocks and clubs. It was too late to escape. A brute of a man, with a bushy, red beard raised his fist and took a swipe at Phileas. It would have landed too if it had not been for Fix who stepped between them. Poor Fix sank to his knees with a huge bruise appearing on the side of his head.

"Yankee!" Phileas glared fiercely at the man.

"An Englishman," the man said. "What's your name? We shall meet again."

"Phileas Fogg. And yours?"

"Colonel Stamp Proctor," came the reply as the crowd swept on once more.

Phileas picked up Fix, who was not badly hurt, and thanked him for his help.

"None necessary," said the detective, "but now can we go?"

At the hotel Passepartout was waiting with half a dozen revolvers he had bought. He bristled on seeing Fix but held his tongue.

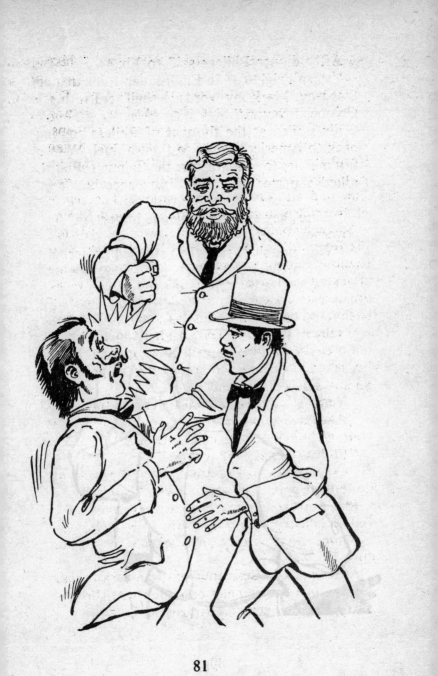

After dinner Phileas said to Fix,

"It isn't right for an Englishman to be treated that way. Mark my words, I shall return to see Colonel Proctor."

Fix smiled at the thought of Phileas coming back to America simply to fight a duel. With a few minutes to spare, before the train left, Phileas asked a porter what the disturbance had been about.

"Were they electing someone important? The governor?"

"Why no, sir," said the surprised porter. "It was for a magistrate!"

Chapter 26
Along the Pacific Railway

San Francisco to New York by railway is exactly three thousand seven hundred and eighty six miles. Before the railway was built, the journey could have taken six months but when President Lincoln gave the go-ahead the steel ribbon started to roll across the plains and mountains. At the height of construction, an amazing one and a half miles of track were being laid every day. Each evening, trains would bring in supplies on rails laid that day for the next day's work.

The carriages had two rows of seats facing front and platforms which enabled passengers to walk the length of the train, visiting saloon bars, restaurants and smoking cars. It did not yet have a travelling theatre but it was surely only a matter of time.

When they left San Francisco it was already cold and miserable. An hour later, a light snow began to fall, covering the countryside in a grey sheet. By eight o'clock most passengers were tired and pleased to see the conductor ingeniously change the carriages into dormitories — benches becoming beds, each with its own, thick curtain for privacy. The next morning, with the carriages returned to normal, they reached the first range of mountains. Smoke from the fat chimney curled up through gigantic fir trees. Shrieks from the engine's whistle drowned out the noise of

waterfalls and raging rivers.

In Nevada, huge herds of buffalo still roamed. In fact at one point the train had to stop completely while ten thousand or more crossed the track. Passepartout wanted the driver to push his way through the herd, knocking them out of their way with the engine's cow-catcher. As usual Phileas calmly took no notice, knowing the buffalo could not be hurried and that force would cause even more delay.

"What a country!" thought Passepartout. "I wonder if Mr Fogg anticipated *this* kind of delay!"

Chapter 27
No-One Listens to Reason

After the Great Salt Lake the track first goes
north and then east between several ranges of
mountains where the engineers had their most
difficult times building the railway. But instead
of spoiling the mountains, they followed the
natural contours and had built only one tunnel
on the whole stretch.

By ten o'clock that night they had reached
Wyoming. It was snowing hard but, mixed with
rain, it was not settling. At the same time as
Passepartout was wishing that Phileas had made
his bet in summer, Aouda was concerned because
she had spotted the red-haired colonel on the
train. While Phileas was asleep Aouda told
Passepartout and Fix what she had seen.

"Don't worry, madam. He first has me to deal
with."

"That's good of you but they mustn't meet."

"You're right," said Fix. "Win or lose, Mr
Fogg would be delayed."

"We must keep him here in the carriage for
the next four days and just hope that chance
doesn't bring them together," said Passepartout.

When Phileas woke, Fix put his plan into
action. He bought two packs of cards and some
counters. With the help of Aouda, they settled
down to play whist.

During the day they travelled through the
Rocky Mountains before descending to a vast,

flat plain crossing all the way to the Atlantic
Ocean. Passepartout at last breathed easily,
feeling that danger was finally behind them.

After breakfast the next day, whist was

resumed. But before one hand was finished the train shuddered to a halt. Passepartout found the train had stopped by a red signal and the station master from Medicine Bow was talking excitedly to the driver and passengers.

"No, no," he was saying, "it's too risky, the bridge ain't going to take the weight." Several cables on the suspension bridge had snapped and it was uncertain that it would hold the train's weight.

"We've telegraphed for a replacement but it's going to be six hours at least."

"Six hours!" cried Passepartout, in dismay.

"Certainly," he was told. "Anyway it will take that long to walk there."

"But it's no more than a mile," someone protested.

"It's too dangerous, we have to detour."

Just then the engineer called out, "Perhaps there is another way to get over, gentlemen."

"On the train? But surely it's not safe!"

"Crossing at full speed, we have a chance."

Passepartout could not believe his ears.

"There is a safer way," he called out.

"The driver says it'll work. Are you afraid?"

"Me, afraid! I'll show you that a Frenchman is every bit as brave as an American!"

Climbing on board, Passepartout could not help thinking his idea of walking across the bridge and letting the train follow, made more sense.

The engineer backed the train a mile or so down the track like a long-jumper. Then with a whistle it moved forward. The pistons worked up and down, gradually picking up speed until they were travelling faster than in all the journey. The driver's notion was that at one hundred miles an hour the train hardly touched the track at all. In a flash they were on the bridge, the train, so to speak, leaping from one side to the other, travelling so fast it took five miles to stop.

But even as they crossed the bridge the cables began to snap, one by one, and the bridge collapsed for ever into the rapids of Medicine Bow.

Chapter 28
Strange Events

As the train relentlessly crossed the country, Phileas, Fix and Aouda continued their cards. Phileas was on the point of playing a spade when a voice behind said,

"Diamonds would be better." Phileas turned to see Colonel Proctor rudely looking over his shoulder.

"Ah, it's the Englishman," said the colonel. Phileas stood up and faced the American. Aouda turned pale. She held Phileas's arm and gently pulled him back as Fix intervened.

"Remember me. I have first shot at you."

"Mr Fix," said Phileas, "this is my business." He turned to the colonel and challenged him to a duel.

"Sir, I seek satisfaction. Unfortunately, I am in a hurry," he said, "but set a time six months in the future and I shall return."

"Make it six years," mocked the American. "The train stops for ten minutes at the next station — plenty of time for a dozen pistol shots."

An hour later, the train's whistle announced they had reached Plum Creek. Phileas stepped off the train but the colonel was prevented by the conductor, waving his arms.

"You can't get off. We're behind schedule and must leave."

"But we're to fight a duel."

"Under any other circumstances I'd be happy to help," the conductor apologised. "I tell you what, why not duel as the train travels?"

Passepartout, amazed by the conductor's

attitude, watched as he led the way to the rear carriage and politely asked the passengers to step outside for a few minutes. Armed with pistols, Phileas and the colonel went in alone.

But as their seconds waited to see who would come out alive, gunshots and wild cries came from the other end of the train. Colonel Proctor and Phileas forgot their differences for the moment and came out to investigate.

"We're under attack from Red Indians!"

Around a hundred Sioux were shooting at the train from horseback. Some had leapt on to the carriages and already the driver and his mate were down and out under blows from tomahawks. The Indians tried to stop the train but, not knowing how, turned the wrong knobs and actually made the engine go faster.

From carriage to carriage they advanced, down the aisles or taking short cuts over the roof. Some carriages were barricaded, with the hope of staying alive until they reached a nearby fort.

By now the conductor, with Phileas, had realised the train was out of control.

"Unless it's stopped in five minutes," he warned, "we'll all be dead."

"I'll go," volunteered Passepartout. Without waiting for an answer he swung down from the carriage platform and began to work his way towards the front, hanging desperately from the underside of the coach. Beneath him, the track rushed by frighteningly. Stones jumped up and stung Passepartout on his face and arms. Without the agility of an acrobat it could never have been done. Little by little, holding on to cables and

brake levers, Passepartout gradually made the
front.

He tried to release the coach connection but
the moving train kept the chain too tight. It
would have stayed that way if they had not hit
an almighty bump that produced enough slack
for Passepartout to get the connector out.

As the coach and engine separated the Indians

took to their heels, frightened away by soldiers from the fort who had finally heard the disturbance and come to the rescue. When the passengers were counted, as well as many injured, three were missing — one of them Passepartout.

Chapter 29
Phileas Does His Duty

Had the three passengers been killed or taken by the Sioux? It was impossible to tell. Aouda was safe and so was Phileas but the detective was slightly hurt and the unpleasant Colonel Proctor was in a bad way, needing help urgently.

Phileas got down from the train, a serious look on his face. Aouda knew what he was thinking. Should he stay and look for Passepartout, risking his wager, or should he go on?

"I will find him," he said, "dead or alive. And, if we start immediately with luck it will be alive."

He turned to the commanding officer and explained about the missing men.

"Will you follow them?" he asked. "Lives are at risk."

"No doubt," said the soldier, "but am I to risk fifty men to save three?"

"You should, sir."

"I don't need you to tell me my duty!"

"Then I'll go alone," said Phileas.

"No, you won't," said the commander, touched by Phileas's bravery. "I want volunteers!" he called to his troops. All of them came forward.

Phileas asked Fix to look after Aouda, who was white with worry. With a squeeze of his hand Phileas said goodbye and a little before noon, rode into the snow; promising a reward of five thousand dollars if the missing passengers were saved.

Around two o'clock a whistle was heard. The run-away engine was returning. After Passepartout released the coaches it had shot along the tracks but, without the fire being fed, it soon ran out of steam and stopped. When the driver and his mate recovered they stoked up and travelled back in search of their missing passengers.

Seeing the engine, Aouda asked the conductor if they would be leaving at once.

"Certainly, madam," he told her. "We are three hours behind schedule. If you want to stay here there'll be another train tomorrow."

Aouda, of course, stayed and so did Fix. Throughout the night, full of sadness, Aouda imagined the worst; dozing and dreaming inside the waiting room.

The soldiers' commander was also worried. Would he have to send another squad to rescue the first? He called a lieutenant and was about to order a reconnaissance when a shot was heard. Signal or an attack? They rushed out to see. A band of men, a good half mile away was being led by Phileas and right behind was Passepartout and the other two missing travellers. The Sioux had been found no more than ten miles away from the fort. Even before the rescue party had arrived Passepartout and his companions had tried to escape, fighting desperately with the Indians. The soldiers had finished the job in double quick time.

Aouda welcomed Phileas and Passepartout

joyfully. As Phileas gave the brave soldiers their
reward, Passepartout shouted in alarm.

"The train! The train!"

"Gone," said Fix.

"What time is the next?' asked Phileas.

"Not until this evening."

"Ah," said Phileas calmly.

Chapter 30
Fix Helps Phileas

"Seriously, Mr Fogg," asked Fix, "are you honestly in a hurry?"

"Certainly."

"Then would you like to know how you can make up the time?"

"On foot?" asked Phileas.

"On a sledge, Mr Fogg," Fix said triumphantly. "On a sledge with sails! Someone I met last night suggested it." Fix pointed out the man and Phileas went over to him.

Phileas agreed a price and with the wind from the west, they set out for Omaha, where they hoped to catch up once more with the trans-America train. What a journey! Skimming over the frozen prairie at forty miles an hour, they felt the cold wind acutely in spite of the heavy furs they wore.

Aouda was protected quite well from the cold, wrapped cosily as she was in furs. Passepartout, though, had no such protection. He was perched on the front of the craft, his face, exposed to the biting wind, glowing as red as the sun. Even so, his spirits were rising again as he thought they might just make the Liverpool steamer. For the first time in a long time he felt kindly disposed towards Fix for having found the only vehicle capable of getting them to Omaha. He also felt strongly attached to Phileas, after all he had risked his fortune to rescue Passepartout from the Indians.

Once or twice, a pack of wolves was spotted, driven by hunger towards the railway track. Passepartout would grip his revolver tighter, ready to shoot if any of them got too brave.

By about noon Phileas knew they were going to beat the deadline.

"There's Omaha," he said. "We've made it!"

Arrived! They had arrived at the station with numerous connections to New York. Their troubles were over.

Passepartout and Fix clambered off. Easing aching muscles they helped Phileas and Aouda and, together, headed for the station. As luck would have it, a train was about to leave for Chicago.

By four o'clock the next afternoon the train reached Chicago, proudly situated on the shore of Lake Michigan. Just nine hundred miles separated them from their ship.

At last, the Hudson River came into view. At a quarter past eleven on the night of the 11th December, the train pulled up before a deserted pier of the Cunard Line.

The *China* had sailed for Liverpool three quarters of an hour before!

Chapter 31
Phileas Challenges His Bad Luck

When the *China* left, it seemed to take
Phileas's last hope. According to his Bradshaw
timetable, no other boat leaving New York would
serve his purpose until the 14th and that was too
late.

Passepartout was crushed. Everything was his
fault. Throughout the journey it had been his
actions that had caused the delays. He would
never forgive himself. As usual though, Phileas
didn't blame anyone.

"Come on," he said, "let's find a hotel and
think what to do tomorrow."

At seven the next morning, Phileas had exactly
nine days, thirteen hours and forty-five minutes
to reach the Reform Club. Leaving the hotel
alone he went straight to the docks. There were
plenty of vessels to hire but mostly sailing ships
and not fast enough. Just about to give up hope,
he spotted a likely-looking one, with smoke rising
from its funnel.

Phileas took a ferry out to the ship.

"Where are you heading for?" he asked the
captain, a big man with skin the colour of copper.

"Bordeaux, in France."

"With cargo or passengers? No? Then will you
take me and three others to Liverpool?"

"I'm going to Bordeaux," said the captain who
hated passengers.

"But what would the owners say?" protested

Phileas.

"I am the owner."

"Then hire it to me."

"No!"

"I'll buy the ship then."

"No!"

For once on this voyage money was not having its usual effect.

"Then will you take us to Bordeaux?"

"No, sir. Not if you paid me two hundred dollars."

"I'll pay two thousand," said Phileas.

"Each?" At that price the captain thought, they were no longer passengers but valuable cargo.

"I start at nine," said Captain Speedy. "Will you be ready?"

"We'll be here," said Phileas, simply, although he had a lot to do in half an hour.

When Passepartout heard what the voyage was costing he groaned aloud. As for Fix, adding up all that Phileas had spent, he was wondering how much of the robbery money would still be left.

Chapter 32
Phileas Rises to the Occasion

At noon the next day, a man went to the bridge
of the *Henrietta* to check their position. It ought
to have been Captain Speedy but it was actually
Phileas. The captain was in his cabin under lock
and key and his angry shouts told everyone that
he was far from pleased.

When Phileas saw that the *Henrietta's* crew was
not a regular one, and not too happy with
Captain Speedy, he formed a daring plan.
Determined to get to Liverpool, he began bribing
the sailors who went over the captain's head and
put Phileas in command.

For several days all went well. Progress was
good and Passepartout got on famously with the
crew. In his cabin, Captain Speedy continued to
howl and Passepartout, when he took the
captain's meals, made sure he kept out of reach.

On the thirteenth the barometer suddenly
dropped, announcing bad weather. The wind
strengthened and swung round, causing them to
take in sail. Phileas ordered the boilers to make
more steam but the long waves, breaking over
their stern, slowed them down.

By the sixteenth they were once more able to
put up the sails. Yet that morning, the chief
engineer warned Phileas that stocks of coal were
dangerously low. Phileas thought for a moment
or two then told the engineer to keep feeding the
boilers until the last lump of coal had gone. Two

days later the engineer announced they'd soon be out.

"Keep stoking till the last," he said, and then called for the captain to be brought up.

As he approached the bridge, Captain Speedy was like a bomb ready to go off.

"Where are we, you pirate?" he thundered.

"Seven hundred miles from Liverpool," Phileas replied coolly. "I have a proposition, Captain. I'd like to buy your ship."

"No, by the devil, she's not for sale!"

"I must tell you," said Phileas, "I shall have to burn her."

"Burn my ship!" screamed the sailor.

"The top half at least. Our coal has run out."

"Burn my vessel, a ship worth fifty thousand dollars?"

"Here are sixty thousand," said Phileas, producing a roll of bank notes with an immediate, calming effect.

"Things could be worse," thought the captain, "the ship is twenty years old so I'm really getting a bargain." The time bomb was not going to explode after all.

"On one condition," said the wily captain. "I get the hull."

"Agreed," said Phileas, giving back half the ship he'd just bought.

Now that the ship was his, Phileas ordered the crew to start cutting down everything above decks made of wood. First the interior seats and bunks went into the furnace. On the next day the masts and rafts went. Passepartout and the crew sawed with all their might. Most of the deck had gone by the twentieth when they sighted the Irish coast. By ten that night Phileas had less than twenty-four hours remaining when a new plan came to him.

"Captain, is that Queenstown, where the mail is dropped?" he asked. Instead of sailing all the way to Liverpool in his ship, Phileas calculated that by taking a train from Queenstown to Dublin and then a faster ship to Liverpool, he could save several hours. And so it was, on the morning of December 21st, that Phileas and his party stood once more on British soil just six hours from London.

"Mr Phileas Fogg," said Detective Fix, "I arrest you in the name of the Queen!"

Chapter 33
Phileas Finally Reaches London

Had he not been restrained, Passepartout would have killed Fix. Instead, he was tortured by his thoughts, knowing that he had not told Phileas about Fix's arrest warrant. Distraught, Passepartout wept till he could not see and wished he could blow his brains out.

Inside the Customs House, Phileas watched the minutes ticking by on his watch. Did he think of escape or ruin? Possibly, but with the door locked and barred he simply took out his diary and wrote 'December 21st, 11.40 a.m. . . .' and waited.

At one o'clock he realised his watch was two hours fast. By express train there was still time. Then outside, he heard Passepartout's raised voice and doors being unlocked. His door swung open.

"Sir," stammered Fix, "forgive me, sir . . . a most unfortunate resemblance . . . three days ago the robber was arrested. You are free to go."

Phileas looked the detective in the eye and then, with possibly the only rapid movement he had made in his life, hit Fix squarely on the chin.

Moments later they were in the station only to find they had missed the express train by five minutes.

"Order me a special train then," demanded Phileas.

Under normal circumstances, five and a half

111

hours would have been sufficient. But with unexpected delays, Phileas arrived in London as the clocks were showing ten minutes to nine.

Having travelled around the world he was behind by five minutes. He had lost the wager.

Chapter 34
Passepartout Does Not Need Telling Twice

Back in London, Phileas sent Passepartout out for some provisions and went to his house in Savile Row. He carried his misfortune with his usual calmness even though, thanks to the blundering of a detective, he was a ruined man. By now his friends at the Reform Club would have cashed his cheque for twenty thousand pounds and there was precious little left from the money he had taken with him.

A room was found for Aouda who was overwhelmed with sorrow at Phileas's problems. Passepartout at last turned off his gas and decided he would need to keep an eye on Phileas in case he did anything silly. The next morning, Passepartout was called to Phileas and told to look after Aouda. He would speak to her that evening but in the meantime was not to be disturbed — he had to put his affairs in order. Passepartout could hold his tongue no longer. Filled with guilt at not having warned Phileas he said,

"Master why don't you curse me? It was my fault that . . ."

"Go," said Phileas calmly, "I blame nobody."

For the rest of that day (Sunday) the house was unusually quiet. For the first time ever, Phileas did not leave at eleven thirty for his club. Why should he? When he had not appeared the night before (Saturday 21st December at a quarter

to nine) he had lost the bet. There was nothing to be said and no reason to go out. Instead, Phileas spent the day locked in his room with Passepartout continually running up and down stairs as his master requested.

At half past seven Phileas went to see Aouda, and sat down opposite her near the fireplace, his face emotionless.

"Aouda, will you forgive me for bringing you to England?" he asked. "When we left your home in India I was a rich man. I planned to use my fortune to make your life free and happy. But now I am ruined."

"No, Mr Fogg," replied Aouda, "I should be asking your forgiveness, for in some small way, I've been the cause of your delay. What will become of you now?"

"I need nothing."

"Your friends will . . ."

"I have no friends," said Phileas. "Nor any relatives."

"I'm sorry for you, Mr Fogg. Everyone should have someone with whom they can share their troubles."

"So they should, Madam."

"In that case, Mr Fogg," said Aouda, rising from the chair and grasping Phileas by the hand, "will you have me for your wife?"

Phileas stood up, his lips trembling slightly. In Aouda's face all he could see was kindness and caring. For an instant he closed his eyes. Opening them he said simply,

"I love you, Aouda. Yes, I love you and am entirely yours!"

Passepartout was called. As soon as he saw Aouda's hand in Phileas's, he understood what had happened and a huge smile crossed his face.

"Is it too late to notify Reverend Wilson this evening?"

"It's never too late for a marriage," smiled Passepartout although his watch showed five minutes past eight. "Will it be for tomorrow, Monday?"

"Yes, tomorrow," cried Aouda. "Now go as fast as you can."

Chapter 35
Once More Phileas is the Talk of the Town

Until a few days earlier, Phileas had been seen by all as a common thief. Then the real bank robber had been captured in Edinburgh and Phileas was once more an honourable man, pursuing an eccentric journey around the world. The papers had resumed their discussion on his chances of success and more side bets had been placed.

Phileas's friends at the Reform Club, who to be honest had forgotten about Phileas, then spent the next few days on tenterhooks. Where was he? Why had no news been received? Would he reappear before the deadline passed?

On the night of the 21st of December a great crowd gathered in Pall Mall, giving the police considerable trouble keeping order. As the clock ticked around to the appointed hour, excitement rose to fever pitch. The five protagonists met in the saloon bar and tried to pass the time, casually playing cards. At twenty past eight Andrew Stuart got up saying,

"Gentlemen, Mr Fogg has exactly twenty-five more minutes left."

"What time did the last train from Liverpool arrive?"

"An hour ago," replied Ralph, "plenty of time to get here."

"In that case," said Andrew, "we can assume the bet is won."

"Not so fast," said Samuel. "Mr Fogg is very punctual."

"The fact is," said Andrew, "that Phileas has lost. The *China* is the only steamer he could have caught and I know for certain he wasn't on it."

The hands of the club clock ticked on. "Five minutes more."

The friends looked at each other. They could hardly hold back their anxiety. Eighteen minutes to nine. The players took up the cards again. Minutes had never seemed longer.

"Seventeen minutes to nine," said Thomas, a perfect silence descending on the club, broken only by the ticking clock.

"Sixteen minutes to nine!" whispered John, his voice cracking with emotion. One minute more and the bet would be won. The group dropped their cards and counted the seconds. At the fortieth second, nothing. At the fiftieth, still nothing. At fifty-five a loud cry went up in the street, followed by rapturous applause. The players rose out of their seats.

At the fifty-seventh second the door of the saloon opened and Phileas Fogg appeared followed by the excited crowd that had forced its way in from the streets. In a calm voice he said,

"Here I am, gentlemen."

Chapter 36
Phileas Wins Nothing but Happiness

When Passepartout had left the Reverend Wilson's house it was eight thirty-five. But what a state he was in; hair a mess, without a hat and running so fast he knocked over several innocent people.

In three minutes he burst into the house in Savile Row.

"Master," he gasped, "marriage impossible — for tomorrow."

"Impossible?" asked Phileas. "Why's that?"

"Because tomorrow is Sunday! You have made a mistake of one day. Today is Saturday! We arrived twenty-four hours early! But now you have only ten minutes left!"

Out in the street Phileas hailed a cab. With the promise of one hundred pounds reward the driver ran over two dogs and overturned several coaches on his way to the club. The clock showed a quarter to nine when they appeared in the great saloon. Phileas had travelled around the world in eighty days and had won the twenty-thousand-pound wager.

But how could a man so careful as Phileas make such a mistake? The answer is simple. We all know that different places in the world have different times. For each of the three hundred and sixty degrees around the circumference of the world, there is a four-minute difference in time. Three hundred and sixty times four minutes

gives precisely twenty four hours. Going eastward, into the rising sun, every day the sun rose a little earlier and time was saved.

After deducting expenses, there was a little over one thousand pounds left of the wager which he divided between Passepartout, first deducting the cost of his gas, and Fix, against whom he bore no grudge.

That evening he asked Aouda,

"Do you still want to marry me?"

"Do you want to marry me?" she replied. "Before, you were ruined, now, you're rich again."

"My fortune belongs to you," said Phileas. "Without your asking me to marry you we'd never have discovered the wrong date until it was too late."

The marriage took place two days later with Passepartout insisting that he had earned the right to give the glowing and dazzling bride away. The next morning, very early, Passepartout knocked on Phileas's door.

"Master," he called, "I've been thinking. We could have done the journey in seventy-eight days!"

"No doubt, but if we had not gone across India I wouldn't have met my darling wife."

Phileas had won his wager. He had used every means of transport and showed marvellous qualities of calmness and bravery. But what then? What had he really gained for his troubles? What had he brought back from a long and difficult journey?

Nothing you might say. Perhaps so. Except,

that is, the love of a charming woman who made Phileas the happiest of men. And surely that alone was worth a tour around the world.